PEEKING THROUGH THE
Pearlies

PEEKING THROUGH THE

Brenda Wilson

READERSMAGNET, LLC

Peeking Through the Pearlies
Copyright © 2017 by Brenda Wilson

Published in the United States of America
ISBN Paperback: 978-1-947765-15-3
eBook: 978-1-947765-16-0

All rights reserved. No part of this publication may be reproduced, stored in a retrieval system or transmitted in any way by any means, electronic, mechanical, photocopy, recording or otherwise without the prior permission of the author except as provided by USA copyright law.

Scriptures marked KJV are taken from *King James Version* (KJV): *King James Version*, public domain.

The opinions expressed by the author are not necessarily those of ReadersMagnet, LLC.

ReadersMagnet, LLC
10620 Treena Street, Suite 230 | San Diego, California, 92131 USA
1.619. 354. 2576 | www.readersmagnet.com

Book design copyright © 2017 by ReadersMagnet, LLC. All rights reserved.
Cover design by Ericka Walker
Interior design by Shieldon Watson

DEDICATION

This work is dedicated to my friend and savior, the Miracle Maker, and my granddaughter Hadley, who at the innocent age of eighteen months stood with both hands firmly planted on either side of a small crack between pocket doors. The expectation of the unknown wonders in the next room illuminated her face as she peeked through the doors into the darkness of the other side. This little miracle let me see how much more we should peer with expectation as we peek through the pearlies into the light.

Her little sister Calloway once asked a little friend if she believed in the wind. The child responded that she did. Calloway then asked if the other little girl had ever seen the wind, and the answer was no. Calloway then wanted to know if the little girl had ever seen what the wind had done, and the answer was yes. And so, it is with child-like belief in the Miracle Maker.

Contents

Foreword 9

Introduction 11
One Winter's Night 13
Remediation 19
In Dreams 23
Fishers of Men 27
Sugar is Sweet 31
Out of the Mouths of Bugs 33
Second Chance 41
Wildflowers 47
Hope 49
Hole in My Head, Lump in My Breast 51

Conclusion 55

Foreword

This little treasure is a great big reminder that miracles still happen; they always have. How do we stop listening and seeing how miraculous God is? This book encourages the reader to hear the way God tries to speak to us. In other ways, it prompts the reader to stay open to God's attempts to speak to others *through* us. The true-to-life stories in this book are exemplary of God's gentle prompting to look for expressions of his love in all of life's moments. No matter how or why our senses are dulled to God's miracles, he is relentless in his pursuit of our attention and affection. Read; listen; enjoy.

—Pashia Groom, Ph.D.

The rarest and truly most cherished experiences in life take many years of living to be realized. It is after these experiences we often lament on not having kept a written record. Compiled in these pages are true stories penned by an author who always remembered when God touched her heart. These are the short stories you will never forget.

—Bud Wilson

Introduction

I HAVE NEVER BEEN a woman of great physical stature. Reaching for a dish on a top cabinet shelf or wanting to wipe clean the top of a windowpane still causes me to lament my constant vertical challenge.

During these golden years of my life, I reflect on the lessons that the life's master has taught to this difficult student. I realize that I have learned yet one more.

You have to be willing to become small like a child. Like a child, you must be able to become humble in a moment. You must blindly believe when the only answer to your question is *because*. You cannot stand so tall that the world obscures your view. You must be fearfully innocent as you peek to see the bows imprisoned in the raindrops, promising showers of miracles that will pour freely from the portals of heaven.

I've spent the last five decades of this life caught in the bustle of everyday living. I searched for the love of a mate, worked for money, and sought knowledge through education. Making my way, I lived a wife's life, reared my children, succeeded in my professional career, and became a very responsible adult.

Wondering about the emptiness of the accomplishments of my spent youth, I now understand that one needs only to find God's child that lives within. Embracing each new day's adventure, viewed through the eyes of this child, anyone can clearly see the miracles.

The following are but a few miraculous accounts. I hope they will encourage you to stand at the gate, while your heavenly Father allows you to peek through the pearlies and shows you a little of the wonder that is yet to come.

One Winter's Night

It had been one of those Midwest winters only outdone by the poles. The snow was heavy, the air wet, and the wind constant, with a bite to the bone. We had more than our share of snow, ice under the snow, ice on top of the show, and ice hanging from every tree bough and power line.

Passing through a door the Lord had opened, this was the year it became possible for me to complete my training as a registered nurse. I was attending a school an hour drive away, and I had not missed a class yet due to the weather.

My family was sacrificing much in the way of finances, plus wife and mother time. Supporting me all the way, my husband was wonderful—he looked after our children and helped get them off in the morning, while I stud ied. Picking up some shifts at the local hospital when I could, I attempted to ease the financial strain. Still, I relished most of the cold nights when I could slip into bed beside my husband after kissing the children good night and soundly sleep in the comfort of my home.

One particular night, I had agreed to work the evening shift. During the night, reports of terrible weather kept coming in. An emergency that occurred late in the shift required my help, and I was unexpectedly detained. It was well after midnight when I started to my car.

The reports of bad weather were understated. I became a believer in the weatherman as I stepped out of the hospital door. Immediately, I was blasted with wind-driven freezing rain. Slipping and sliding, I made my way to the car. I only had nine blocks to go, and then I would be safe and warm in my house with my family. I clung to the car the best that I could and relentlessly worked until I could get my door open. I fell inside and started the little Ford Pinto. My next chore would be dreadful. Reluctantly, I left the shelter of the little car and hesitantly stepped out in the torrent of stinging ice needles. I began chipping at the ice covering the windshield and passenger window. I had to be able to see just a little. Finally, bones aching from the teeth of the wind, my face and eyes stinging from the little darts, I created a peek hole that I would make suffice. Once back in the driver's seat, I welcomed the bit of warmth coming from the heater.

I nudged the little car out of its parking space onto the glazed road and decided that maybe this wasn't going to be such a big deal after all. I held onto that reassuring thought, as my eyes beheld the first stop sign. Gently tapping the brake as I had many times before when driving on ice, I proceeded at a snail's pace. My little car skated right on through the intersection without hesitation.

I could find my way to and from the hospital blindfolded and knew any approach I made to my house consisted of passing through a less desirable part of town, railroad tracks, and a huge hill. If I could just navigate the crest of the hill, the rest of my journey would be short. I would finally be home.

Just beyond the railroad tracks that crossed my path, straight ahead began the swell of the iced mountain that I had to conquer.

Determined to reach my destination, I accelerated just a little to get some momentum for the climb. Feeling that the rear of the car was starting to mimic a fish, I cautiously pressed onward. A little less than halfway up the hill, tires singing with the forward rotation, I felt the car slipping backward. Coming to a rest on the wrong side of the tracks, I became more determined than ever to get to my house and began the process again. It was after my third backward trip down the hill that I began to fear I would spend the night right in the middle of the road. It was then when I saw a blue glow slide to a stop beside my car. I cracked my window just a little and peered into the face of one of the local police officers. Tipping his hat to me, he said, "Ma'am, this really isn't a very safe neighborhood for you to be alone in."

I replied, "Yes, sir, I know. I just need to get over the top of this hill, and I'll almost be home." I smiled, thinking he might offer to help.

He touched his hat once again, saying, "You be careful, hear!" He rolled up his window and slid away.

A little nudge with his bigger car would have been nice, I though, understanding why he wouldn't want to get out and push in this mess.

With the heavy darkness settling around me, I began to feel desperate. I realized the freezing rain was increasing in intensity to the point that my windshield was rapidly becoming covered in spite of the wipers and the defroster. I knew there would be no other rescuer, for no one would venture out in this.

Tears welled up in my eyes and threatened to freeze while sliding down my cheeks. I resolved to make one more attempt. "Please, God," I prayed, "just help me get home."

I challenged the hill one more time and stepped down on the accelerator. At the halfway mark, I felt the car start backward. I stomped hard on the brake and the car stopped. Simultaneously, I heard a pecking sound on the side window. I was sure the rain was now hail, until I turned and saw a black figure standing beside my car. Barely creating a slit in my window, I heard a reassuring voice call out, "When I say go, I'll push and you give it all you've got."

Grateful for the help, I waited for the command and did as I was told. The little car scaled the iced mountain and topped the crest as if it were moving on dry pavement. I rolled my window all the way down and stuck my head out, shouting my gratitude to this kind person. My words were forever lost in the wind, for no figure was to be seen.

Not one to waste a good deed, I made my way to my driveway. Eagerly stepping out of the car, I abruptly found myself sitting on the ground. I crawled across the glassed yard, up our steps, and finally dragged myself through my back door. Home at last! It wasn't until I had kissed my children and crawled into bed beside my husband that I began to ponder just what had happened.

In desperation, I had asked God for help, my car had stopped on a glacier, and an unknown figure had stood beside my car, maintained enough traction to shove me the rest of the way up and over the top of the mountain, then disappeared. I remembered not being able to stand. I remembered crawling to my house and wondered if I had been visited by an angel unaware or if this had just been some extremely sure-footed, able-bodied Good Samaritan.

I no longer seek the answer to that question but will forever carry the lesson learned with me. It doesn't matter how large the obstacle. When I have tried all, I know what to do and cry out to God in honest desperation, he will hear me. I am never alone. If I will listen for his command, he will push if I will give it all that I have. There is no mountain we can't climb.

Remediation

IT WAS AN UNUSUALLY gentle day. The breeze was balmy; the radiant sunshine was warm, and love was in the air. I hoped it was. Our family's Beagle-Basset dog, Tuffy, had been missing almost a month. Our five-year-old daughter and three-year-old son had grieved every day of the month. Even on this day, they had faithfully put out food and water through a short burst of tears.

We hadn't received any response from the newspaper and radio ads we'd placed for our lost furry friend. My husband drove the neighborhood every evening. We hoped he might spot a passionate Tuffy visiting a lady friend, bring the dog home, and end our children's sorrow. I hoped with all my heart that this evening would be the night that Tuffy would be found.

Church and Sunday school had become an important part of our daughter's life of late. The children spent many hours playing church in their room. Most times my daughter assumed the role of pastorate and delegated the duty of song leader to her younger brother. Earlier in the afternoon, the play church pastor and the younger song leader came into the kitchen and asked me, "Mama, why doesn't God show Tuffy the way home?"

I thought for a moment and tried to teach a lesson in trust, while I prepared them for the worst and most probable scenario. I shared God's promise that whenever two of his children pray about something, he hears that prayer. I also explained that God does not always answer our prayers when or in the way we think he should. We just have to trust that God knows what is best. I was satisfied that the children understood that if it was God's plan, we would get Tuffy back; and if we didn't, we had to trust that God knows best. I hoped that this would give them some consolation, as I watched my sad children somberly return to the playroom.

I returned to the kitchen to wash the dishes and was gazing out my kitchen window, feeling pretty good about our little chat. Contemplating what I could fix for my hungry husband, so we could eat quickly, and he could get on with the search, I was startled at a loud *thump, thump, thump!*

My two children, heads high, purposefully swinging their arms at their sides, came marching through the kitchen headed toward our back door.

Curious, I asked, "Where are you going?"

"We are going to get Tuffy," my daughter announced.

Fearful for their impending disappointment, I reminded her that Tuffy was still gone. I asked her what made her think he was in the backyard.

Confidently, she replied, "We prayed and asked God to bring Tuffy home, and now we are going out to get him." Without a blink of her eye, a waiver in her voice, or a hesitation in her step, they marched on.

It wasn't the beautiful day or food that I thought about as I watched my children march around the garage, into the side yard, and disappear behind the grapevines.

"Oh, Lord. How will I get myself out of this one?" I muttered under my breath as I shoved my hands into the hot, soapy dishwater. *What maternal words of wisdom can I speak that will make this seem right to my children when they don't find their dog?*

I stood peering out the window, dreading to see the two downcast faces of my defeated children, when what to my disbelieving eyes appeared but, our family's favorite fur person. A low-slung, caramel and white Beagle-Basset cur came running into the backyard from nowhere.

Oh, me of little faith? Lest you have childlike faith. I can still hear my children's joyful shouts of glee upon finding their old friend.

Over the last three decades when life has dropped me to my knees, I immediately seek a prayer partner, remember the lesson that I learned on that day, see the faces of my children, and rejoice in God's abounding faithfulness and love.

In Dreams

KEEPING UP WITH MY husband's voracious appetite for spiritual growth was impossible for me. I watched as he studied his Bible, read Bible commentaries, and researched every sermon we heard on Sunday mornings.

It wasn't that I didn't want to participate in these activities with the same exuberance as my husband, but as a wife and mother of two small children, I did well to keep clothes clean, meals prepared, and dishes washed. I'd post Bible verses around the house so I could read them as I went about my day and stole moments of personal devotional time after everyone was in bed.

Friends of ours often commented, saying, "I wouldn't be surprised if your husband is called to the ministry someday."

To even consider such a possibility froze my heart in fear. I certainly didn't consider myself worthy of the position of a pastor's wife. I thought of our present pastor's wife—perfectly groomed, calm, filled with grace and love—everything I thought a pastor's wife should be.

I remembered the day I greeted our pastor at our door with a babe on one hip, dirty water marks down the front of my legs from scrubbing the floor, soapsuds in one hand, and baby food peaches in the other. Somehow, I just couldn't merge that image with the image of our pastor's wife.

Months went by, and my husband's interest seemed to include a great deal more of information about missions. I really began to worry. I could just envision an altar call to the mission field; my husband answering it, and there I would be. Not only would I be humiliated as a poor role model, but I might be expected to pick up my two babies and go to some danger-laden foreign land. Try as I might, I just couldn't find any peace about this situation.

One night, as I restlessly slipped into deep sleep, I was forced to deal with my dilemma in a strange dream. I dreamed that the Lord was coming to visit my house. The house in the dream made our real home seem immaculately organized. In the dream, I worked in a hurry to get the house ready for this special guest. Strangely enough, when he arrived, he stood on the porch and called our family outside. I heard him ask my husband to go to South Africa for his cause and to be prepared to leave in three days. Soft strains of the old hymn *Just As I am* filled my nightmare. I knelt and pled with the Lord to send my husband. I assured him I would follow but to please give me time to find a safe place for our children to stay behind.

As surely as if someone had spoken aloud, I heard, "If I so choose, I can call my children home any time—if they are in your house, sitting by you in a pew, or in the jungles of Africa. These children you call yours are mine. I have allowed you to know them. As surely as I have loaned them to you, I can keep them wherever they may be." I awoke from the dream with a peace and reassurance that would stay with me.

Several months later we had a young missionary couple come to our church. On their last night, they offered an invitation to people who might be willing to train and go to the field. I felt my husband beside me shift his weight and thought for sure he would step forward. The organist began playing *Just as I am*. I looked down at my innocent children and knew with certainty that if the Lord called we would go. To date, my husband still studies and grows his spiritual life, but he has never felt the call to full-time ministry.

I learned through a dream that the Lord truly will take and keep us just as we are. If He needs us to be something different, He will make a way. It is not always the completion of a task that He calls us to, but it is our willingness to go and do His will that is important. Though I have never served on a foreign mission field or served as a pastor's wife, God gave me peace through the dream, and I knew if called, I would go.

Fishers of Men

Rolling Missouri hills, multiple creek beds, and ponds provided my father-in-law many hours of sport throughout his lifetime, as he hunted, trapped, and fished. His passion for these hobbies was soon to be a driving force of our young son.

My husband had been strongly encouraged to go on many such trips while growing up, but after serving in Vietnam, he had lost any strong desire to hunt or spend much time fishing. Our son, however, found Grandpa's undivided attention to him on a proper way to catch a fish irresistible. Soon our three-year-old had caught his first two-pound catfish. He was forever hooked.

Surrendering to our son's pleas to go fishing, our family often spent part of Saturdays at the lake or on a pond bank. My husband and our daughter often went off exploring, and my son and I were left to catch the fish.

Many times at his tender age of three I have watched him don his fishing hat, an old one of Grandpa's with a few old lures hooked into it, cast his line, hunker down on the bank, and wait for that little nibble with the patience and perseverance of any old salt. Before long, my son was insisting that he wanted to get rid of the red and white bobber on his line. He wanted a weight, set appropriately to catch the biggest fish, in the deepest water, on the bottom.

It was on one such weekend several years later that we were camping on the bank of the Des Moines River with some friends. Fishing, then chasing and playing, the children were having a great time. The adults had laid the firewood and the other works for a wiener roast later that evening, and I had taken the opportunity to do a little fishing of my own. Unlike my husband and daughter, I really liked to fish and found my son an excellent excuse to do just that.

Leaning against a tree twisted by the river's character over many years, I case my line into the frothy, rambling river. I studied the shape of the tree and wondered how long it had stood and how many more years it would stand after I left its shelter. Delighting in the children's noise resounding behind me, I let my gaze wander to a lone man below, walking the edge of the river, snagging for spoonbill. This is a fishing technique where you throw treble hook on the end of a line and jerk it along the edge of the bank, hoping to snag a large fish with a mouth that looks like a flat bill. I never thought it held much sport.

I was lured back to the issue at hand by a *tap, tap, tapping* on my line as some curious fish tested the bait at the other end. Eagerly, I waited for the much-firmer tug that told me it was time to set the hook.

"Catching anything?" my now six-year-old son asked me, grinning from ear to ear. I figured he would ask if I had remembered to spit on the worm, a strange ritual that he and Grandpa had started.

I set the hook and began reeling my catch to shore. Suddenly, I realized that my line was being pulled upstream. The power on the other end was wrapping my rod and me around the tree. The sound of the reel's clutch was singing in my ears until I heard my son yell, "You give that back!" It's not yours! That's my mama's fish."

I watched as my six-year-old fearlessly bolted down the riverbank toward the man snagging at the river's edge and defended my right to the catch. I watched as the man continued to drag my line with my fish on it to shore. I could not hear any further exchange of words, but my son came strutting up the hill with my catch in hand, holding it just the way Grandpa had taught him.

Many times, I have chuckled as I've recanted this tale, but there is a much more important story to be told here. I cannot help but think of my son's heart as he so bravely retrieved what he knew was mine. Recalling how very satisfied he looked as he anticipated my approval for what he had just accomplished. I hope I let him know just how wonderful he was to me. I remember how this parent's heart had thrilled at this young man's character at such an early age. Fearlessly, bravely, boldly he had stood for what he knew was right.

I have been told that if I do certain things I will be made a fisher of men. Spiting on worms is not required, but believe is. In the later years of my walk with the Lord, I have wondered, *Have I been satisfied with just fishing on the surface? Have I dared to give up my bobber to fish the deep water and reach out to someone who believes he is hopelessly at the bottom of his life? Have I been sensitive to the nibble of someone testing the unconditional love of the Lord? Have I known when to set the hook and introduce them to my friend? When the world would snag them and draw them back down, do I run fearlessly, bravely, boldly forward with the heart of a child, declaring that this soul is my father's?*

Sugar is Sweet

On a lazy Saturday afternoon, while spending girl time with my young daughter, I decided to do some baking from scratch. Now in my kitchen, that can be a challenge, and not just because of my height. My assignment that day was sugar cookies.

Attempting to look like a mother who dutifully did her share of baking, I set about making sure we had all of the ingredients we would need before starting our venture. We had flour, eggs, and vanilla extract, and I was sure a five-pound bag of sugar still resided unopened on the Lazy Susan corner cabinet.

Asking my daughter to retrieve the bag of sugar, I set about prioritizing the other ingredients. I made sure that the cookie sheets were clean and the oven was warming to just the right temperature.

Eagerly my five-year-old daughter set about sifting the measured-out flour into my grandmother's old blue crock bowel. Learning to crack eggs was the next culinary lesson in baking. Using my favorite spatula, she meticulously scraped the measured shortening into the blue bowl, and we added a few more small ingredients.

Looking to add the final item, we discovered that the sugar was like a rock. Lugging the concrete five-pound bag became more than my little baker could muster, so I hurried to the rescue and set the sugar on the table. Seeing the furrowed brow and turned-down mouth, I assured my little one we could still bake the cookies. I gave her a spoon and let her begin chipping and scraping away at the sugar mountain. She diligently dug away while I went about the kitchen completing other tasks.

After a while, I went over to check on the progress, only to be surprised at how little loose sugar was in the bag. It was then I saw the telltale crystals about my little girl's mouth. Asking her why she had what looked like sugar around her mouth, she smiled and replied, "Mama, no matter how old the sugar gets, it never loses its sweet."

For some unknown reason, my daughter's comment brought to my mind the title of the old gospel song, "Tis so Sweet to Trust in Jesus."

Whenever I hear the name of the Miracle Maker softly spoken or have the chance to share with someone who doesn't know the story of his unconditional love for me, I take time to pause and remember, "No matter how old the sugar gets, it never loses its sweet." The gift of being able to trust in the Miracle Maker is the sweetest thing I know.

Out of the Mouths of Bugs

Nothing could have prepared my husband and me for the unexpected turmoil that would shake up our comfortable lives the year our daughter turned fourteen.

Our church family had hit a rough patch. Our pastor and friend had left our church, and hard feelings had found a home within the congregation. We had quietly started attending another church, not wanting to be a part of this painful experience. Our closest friends in Christ had answered a call to serve in another church in another state. They took with them their children, some of our daughter's closest friends. After long discussions, my children and I decided we would keep them in the Christian Academy at our old church and see what the Lord would lead us to do.

Our delightful little girl was growing into a lovely young lady with a strong desire to play the piano. She had been taking lessons and progressing well. Her piano teacher encouraged me to find another instructor who could take her to a higher level of training. Following her recommendation, I contacted a music teacher at the public school. Our daughter was accepted, and so the lessons continued.

One evening after her piano lesson, our daughter shared that her piano teacher had a son just a year older who attended the Christian Academy as well. It wasn't long until most of the phone calls at our house were for our daughter. Shortly thereafter, I began receiving calls on the evenings of piano lessons from the teacher to see if our daughter could stay to have supper with the young man and his mother. Since our daughter had always been responsible and knew that any dating consideration was out of the question, I felt this chaperoned socialization was a reasonable compromise. We in turn would, on occasion, invite this young man to share a meal with us or accompany us on a family outing.

Soon the phone calls reached a frequency of frustration for the rest of the family and had to be limited. A noted change was taking place with our daughter. Our outgoing social butterfly was withdrawing from her friends, shunning her younger brother, and skirting private time with her father and me.

Attempting to reconnect with our oldest, we planned a family vacation out of state. During that short time, it was wonderful to see the child we had always known resurface.

Thinking that the ongoing friendship with the young man was more than our daughter was ready to handle, we took a parenting option and dramatically limited the number of phone calls and social time for the two. Surprisingly, this was met with little resistance from our daughter.

Return to our work routines after the vacation, we were relieved to see that our daughter continued to be more like her old self. It was on just such a routing day that I received a call at work from my husband, asking if I had seen our daughter. This was an odd question, since she would have needed to walk several miles to reach my place of employment. Shaking with fear, I could barely hold the phone as he told me he had gone to pick up our children for lunch and our daughter had not returned from a planned bike ride with a girlfriend. Now in the middle of the afternoon, he had contacted everyone he could think of, including the young man and his mother. No one had seen her. The girl she was to meet told him our daughter had never arrived.

Rushing home, I could barely breathe. The gaping hold torn in my maternal heart by fear refused to be filled with my constant pleading with God or by me rationally thinking that she would be waiting for me when I reached our house. Deafening silence greeted me as I stepped through our front door. Looking at my husband and son, I saw the terror in their eyes reflecting what I was feeling. We made the necessary phone call to the police. This began some of the longest hours of my life.

Once word went out over the police scanners in our tri-state area, people began coming by the house and calling briefly to let us know they were looking and praying. Unknown to us, our old pastor was attending a Southern Baptist convention and had asked the many men of God to pray on our daughter's behalf. Three pastors from our community came to the house and prayed with us. A dear friend came to stay by me, while the men and my son went searching. Hours crawled by and the night grew darker with no word about our daughter. In the belly of my soul I was certain this young man and his mother were somehow involved. Still, there was the fear that some crazed pedophile had snatched her.

In the privacy of our bedroom, I remembered my dream of earlier years, knelt, and wept to God. "I know she is yours. Please put your hedge of protection about her. If we're not worthy to have her returned to us and your plan is to call her home, please do so quickly. Don't let her suffer. I give her up to you."

Like a slug, the black night slithered on. The men continued their search. Phone calls came from the police asking verification about what our daughter had been wearing. As the hours passed and there was still no trace of her, I dreaded the call that would come, wanting us to identify her body.

In the wee hours of the morning, a call came from the police requiring our presence at the police station. I explained that my husband was still out searching. I left a note and sent another friend to find my husband and direct him to the police station.

Fear made me feel ill and faint. I wasn't sure I could make this journey. My friend at my side, the Lord as my strength, I put one foot in front of the other and started for the lion's den.

It was not my daughter's corpse or her that awaited me at the police station. There in an interrogation room sat the young man and his mother. Feeling like a spectator, I watched and listened as the police asked them question after question. My husband arrived, and I shared with him that I was more certain than ever that these two knew where our daughter was.

Eventually, the police prepared to let the woman and her son go home. Standing at the front door of the police station, an officer admonished them to be available for later in the day. The two had not reached their car when another officer came running from the back of the station, shouting, "Bring them back in here!" He turned to us and said, "We have your daughter in the back."

Rushing into a report room of the police station, my husband and I embraced our living, breathing daughter. Hair disheveled with bits of fiberglass clinging to it, tiny cuts over her arms, hands and bare feet, tear tracks streaking her dirty face, she was as wonderful to look upon as the first time I held her. After giving statements to the police, we went home. The four of us shared a breakfast of donuts and hot chocolate. The obvious love between our children did more to warm my heart than any hot drink ever could.

Safe in the sanctuary of our home, we asked our daughter to share what had happened. Recounting the story from the beginning, she told us that she had been locked in an unfinished room in an attic. There had been no windows, so the little room had been totally dark. Her shoes had been taken from her. She had tried to get a little door open numerous times. She had shouted for help until her young captor had loaded a rifle and threatened her. Not realizing night had fallen, she had heard cars passing in the street outside and knew people were looking for her. She had sat with her knees to her chest, arms around her legs, and head down for a long time. It was in the silence of her dark little prison she heard the voice of a cricket on the other side of the little door. Grateful for the sign of any other living creature, she had focused on the voice coming out of freedom. Listening intently, the voice seemed to be saying to her, "Leave now."

Recalling the Bible story of Paul being released from prison, she uncurled her arms and crawled over the rafters toward the little door. Her hand found a small board that would later be identified as a scrap piece of shimmed lathe. Reaching the little door, she leaned against it and saw a sliver of light from the room beyond. Still the little bug's voice called to her from the room on the other side. Slipping the small end of the board into the light, she pushed with her shoulder and pried until she could move the board up the side of the door. The cricket's voice grew more intense. The tip of the board came up hard against the latch her captor apparently had failed to secure tightly. The little door burst open, the cricket sang, and our daughter fled down the stairs, out the door, and into the freedom of the night.

A police officer cruising the area spotted her running toward the public park, which was a shortcut to our house. Identifying himself, he called to her, put her in the patrol car, and safely delivered her to us. Washing over me like waves from a distant sea, feelings of the old terror surface each time I hear a new Amber Alert or see some family pleading for the safe return of a missing child. I pray for them, knowing just how blessed we were. I know how different the outcome might have been.

We left our home, school, church, and jobs and began a trek into the wilderness to maintain sanity and protect our daughter. Unfortunately, little justice was served in this realm. Still, God can take the most difficult of circumstances with all of the world's ugliness and create something good. Little did this boy or his mother ever imagine that out of our daughter's experience would emerge a most talented counselor who has a gift for reaching the dark places of abused women and children and helping them heal.

Even now, hearing the songs of the crickets in the still of the evening, I remember my long night. I recall my strange dream from before, and I thank God for his faithfulness. I rest in the assurance that my children, although they are grown with babies of their own, are in his care, and I don't have to be there for them to be protected. He has the entire world at his command and can even use the voice of a bug to call his children out of danger if need be.

Second Chance

RIDING THE TAILWIND OF a wickedly bitter winter, balmy days has brought the families of robins back to the Midwest, and with them the promise of spring. Taking up residence on the protruding logs of our home, they built new nests and officially reopened our bird hotel. It was common for the top four logs to house the nests that held the eggs where mothers sat until at last we heard the *cheeping* of the babies.

On such a spring evening, while vising a friend, my husband and I noticed thunderheads building in the west. Leaving windows of the house open to let spring in had seemed like a good idea when we had left the house. The threat of rain dictated that we hurry home to put the windows down. Upon arriving in our driveway, great drops of rain began coming down in a torrent, and before we could get to the back door it was pouring buckets.

As I paused to open the gate to the breezeway leading to our back door, I saw a tiny orange ball, flecked with white and topped with a brilliant yellow color, outlining a tightly closed beak. Since this tiny robin was sitting in the open with his beak pointing straight up, I feared he would drown in the d deluge of water. I remembered an old wives' tale that says birds gaze upward at falling rain until they drown. Calling to my husband, I asked what I should do with this baby. We were both getting wetter by the minute. My husband firmly suggested that I should just leave things alone and get in out of the rain myself. He allayed my fear by reassuring me that the little bird could find shelter under a leaf or a flower plant nearby or mother robin, not being far away, would certainly tend to her young bird if we would get out of her way and not touch the baby. Miserably wet and getting cold, I dashed through the gate, entered the house and headed for a nice hot shower.

Following a good night's sleep, I dressed, ate breakfast and left for work. Opening the gate of the breezeway, I looked down and felt a wrenching in my heart. There sat the little ball of orange, just as I had abandoned it and left it to weather the storm alone. The eyes were tightly clenched, and not a flutter could be detected beneath the little speckled breast.

When I reached my office, I contacted my husband and asked him to please bury the little bird before I got home from work. I didn't want to see the reminder that I had taken the easy road, and because I did, I would never hear the song that little bird had to sing. I could have moved the flower pot closer to him so the leaves sheltered him. It had been I who had seen the little bird, I who had felt compelled to take some action to protect him, and I, who already wet and cold, chose to seek my own comfort at the urging of a well-meaning husband. It was I who had not listened to the voice in my heart, and because of that, the little bird died and our yard would be quieter this spring.

Arriving home from work, I saw that my husband had completed his good deed and no trace of the little bird remained. Weeks passed, and being a rational, responsible adult, I didn't dwell on the baby robin. However, each time I saw a robin in our yard, an unbidden image of the lifeless little bird would cross my mind. I would flinch with the prick of guilt, swallow hard, and pretend I didn't notice.

During late spring, my husband and I were returning from the store when, true to Midwestern weather, a storm blew up. The straight winds were unusually cold for this time of year, and they drove rain like nails through the trees. Arriving in our driveway, we noted that someone else's trashcan was in our yard and our patio furniture was missing. I opened my door on the passenger side, planning to make a run for the breezeway and the warmth and safety of our home. Stepping out of the car, I looked down to be sure I straddled the puddle of water gathered there, and could hardly catch my breath. There in the black liquid lay not one, but two little shapes. Four bulging eyes covered with gray membrane assured me that these were very young birds. The unremarkable feathers of very young hatchlings covered both bodies. I could hear my husband calling to me to hurry in the house. I could not just walk away this time. I called to him to bring me something we could put two birds in. He returned with a basket and an umbrella.

On closer inspection, it became obvious that only one little breast fluttered with the beating of the heart beneath it. We moved the little dead bird out of the puddle until it could be buried. I then headed to the house with the basket and the sorrowful little life so near its end. My husband brought new shop cloths from the garage, and I warmed them in the microwave. We wrapped the little body in the warm cloths and place the basket on the mantle of the fireplace to keep the family cat at bay.

I felt sure I would find the little bird dead when I check in the morning, but I slept well that night knowing that I had tried by best to help.

Rising bright and early, I wanted to get the chore of taking care of the bird's body over with. I opened the parcel of shop cloths. Staring up at me were two coal-black eyes. Okay, we had made it through the night. Now what? Baby birds have to be fed often. This baby was so young we could not tell for sure what kind of bird it was. I wasn't sure what baby birds ate. I did know it was going to need to be fed and soon. Since birds eat earthworms, which are a high percentage of protein, and cat food is high in protein, I decided I could make gruel of cat food and get by until we could figure something better.

Taking a small blue ear-irrigating syringe, I sucked up a small amount of cat food gruel. I had to pry the little bird's beak open and squirt the gruel down its gullet. This I did faithfully every two hours.   Thriving on the gruel, the little bird began to respond to the ear syringe much like other birds respond to their mother's beak. Screech (that's what we named him) continued to grow. His feathers changed. He outgrew the baskets we had, so we borrowed a birdcage. My husband took to taking the birdcage to the backyard and leaving it there. Soon other black birds, known as starlings, would gather around the cage then fly away when we would retrieve Screech for the night.

Time passed, Screech grew, and we were well into summer. My husband took Screech and his cage to the yard with the intent of cleaning it. He recalled hearing the chattering of other birds in the trees when he sat the cage down. Upon opening the cage door, Screech immediately hopped out and took off across the yard. Following in rapid pursuit, my husband tried earnestly to catch the dependent bird. Suddenly, his task became much more difficult as the adult birds began diving and swooping at my husband's head.

Realizing that this might be a rescue attempt on the big bird's part, my husband retreated to the deck and watched. The adult birds circled Screech, and when they took to the trees, Screech went with them.

The rest of that summer and fall we delighted in watching a large starling with a half-grown fledgling trailing along behind. It was obvious that the fledgling was being taught to find food on its own, a skill young birds learn at a much earlier stage of development. For the next several springs, when the birds returned, we would find a large starling sitting on our deck, screeching as if for food.

Every spring when I see the robins and the starlings, I remember the little ones that touched my life. One a beautiful songbird, the other not so pretty or so well respected, both special, living creations of God. I think of the one lost by in indifference and am grateful that God is long-suffering with his children and that we are all precious in his sight and that even when I don't get it right the first time, he gives me a second chance.

Wildflowers

During the time our church family was torn with conflict and our dearest friends in Christ moved to another state, I found a card to go with their going-away gift. The essence of the verse has stayed with me. The verse told how God spread the seed of his wildflowers upon the wind, so other parts of the earth might see his beauty. Seeing wildflowers in a field, on a hillside, or wherever they might bloom always comforts my heart.

My husband of many years and I were struggling through the empty-nest syndrome. Both of our children were off into the world to make their own lives. Left with the family cat and dog, we worked at getting reacquainted and settling into different roles. No one had prepared me for how difficult and sometimes painful this process could be.

We slowly made our way back to each other. It was during one of the roughest times that I felt a tremendous need to be able to draw comfort from my own patch of wildflowers. I purchased a large bag of seed, and as things sometimes go, spring turned to summer, summer to fall, fall to winter, and the seed still lay in the sack in our garage. The following spring, I discovered the bag of seed and set about preparing a space in the hard earth of the yard. I sowed my seed. Commenting at work about planting wildflower seeds I had purchased the year before immediately met with disbelief and teasing from some of my fellow employees. They assured me that if the seeds were a year old there would be no way they would produce flowers. It wasn't a big deal to me, but I certainly felt the fool in front of my coworkers.

Not having any fresh seed to sow, I figured that the flower bed would just have to lay dormant another year and went about my life. With the spring came the usual rains and warm sunny days. On just such a day, I walked past the intended wildflower garden and thrilled at seeing tender green shoots pushing their way to the sun. Several weeks passed. Soon I gazed upon the beauty of my full-to-overflowing wildflower bed. For the next five years, when I delighted in my flowers, I remembered and gave thanks. My husband and I now thrived in a relationship much richer than before. I remembered our friends who grew tremendously in their work for the Lord. I learned that when we plant a seed in faith, even though it may seem old or stale, even though we may seem foolish to others, with God's rain those seeds tossed on the winds of disparity can flourish, reach for the Son, and bring forth great beauty and comfort.

Hope

Winter has never been my favorite season. Living still in a part of the country where it becomes gray and cold, I always feel the chill of the ice in my heart. It has always been a hard time of the year for me to remain cheerful, even though I know spring will come.

It was late in winter, and early one evening as I arrived at work and stepped out of the car, I was hit with a blast of winter wind and snow. This turned my gray mood to black, since I convinced myself that spring was just days away. Skimping on security lights was not one of the faults of my employer, and I was grateful to be able to see and navigate around the patches of ice that remained from the last winter storm.

Pulling my coat tighter about me, I put my scarf over my head and started across the parking lot toward the steps leading to the back door. The first two steps required caution because of their ice covering; I kept my eyes down and prepared to take the third. I could hardly believe what I was seeing. Sprouting from a crack in the concrete step that was covered with ice except for a small space bloomed a petunia. It was as white as the driven snow. Watching the full blossom bow and bend in the winter wind, I felt my heart begin to melt and my soul warm. I saw that even in the bone-chilling valley of winter, God gave me hope for the coming spring. How wonderful it is to know that even in the grip of death, God sent his Son to bring us hope for eternal life.

Hole in My Head, Lump in My Breast

'TWAS THE SEASON TO be jolly, and we were. Following the Christmas tradition, we had gathered as many of the family as possible around our table to enjoy the ritual Christmas feast. My husband and son had retrieved my Alzheimer's-smitten mother from the nearby care center, and having completed the rite of passage, my daughter-in-law assisted in placing the carved turkey, dressing, homemade noodles, broccoli-and-cheese casserole, green bean casserole, cranberry salad, and scalloped corn on the festive table. We all knew that homemade pie was waiting for desert.

My husband returned grace. I looked around the table as my family and friends began to fill their plates, eager to partake of the holiday feast. Reaching for my own portion of goodies, I began realizing what a relaxed holiday this was. The usual scurrying about at the last minute really didn't occur this day, and I was so grateful.

My world began to swirl as I raised my head from my plate-directed gaze, looked at my daughter-in-law and started to speak. The whirling stopped me midsentence. Being a nurse, I was sure that the searing pain of an aneurysm or unconsciousness would follow. I directed my eyes back to my plate and sat very still. Everything appeared normal. No one else was making a sound. They were watching me. I lifted my eyes toward my daughter-in-law and immediately jumped back on the carnival ride. This time I was very nauseated.

Grabbing for my husband's arm, I murmured, "Get me downstairs. I'm really sick!" Rising from my chair, we realized I wasn't tracking very well. My husband sat me down on the nearby couch. I was sure this was a cerebral vascular incident—a stroke, an aneurysm, maybe even a tumor. A continual torrent of tears trailed down my cheeks. I became more and more agitated at my inability to stay the flow. Now, anyone who knows me also knows I don't do crying very well. I always saw tears as a sign of weakness in myself. But that day, I continued to cry in the absence of pain or fear or sorrow.

Following a trip to the local emergency room, several visits to several specialists, and a multitude of tests, it was decided that I had suffered a stroke in the area of the midbrain. My symptoms in the next few weeks were typical of a stroke but unusually vague. I was left with a very slight weakness in my right hand and uncontrollable crying for no reason. I became grateful for the medication that stayed the flow of tears.

Near the end of this loss of control, although released to go back to work, I found myself without a job. My position had been eliminated. Interesting timing, but leaving me without work just the same.

Having met the deductible on my insurance I decided to complete my annual well-woman exam. This included a mammogram. I had never had a problem and no family history of breast cancer, so I didn't give this a second thought. Imagine the jolt I felt when I received the phone call telling me I needed to repeat the mammogram on my left breast due to a suspicious area.

Now I had a new and very real reason to cry, but did not because of the medication. It was a very strange journey that I was taking. While I was sitting at home waiting for the results of the second mammogram, I thought about Christmas Day and everything that had occurred since.

A hole in my head and a lump in my breast, now what do I do? Now that was catchy little phrase. I thought of the people I had taken care of with a mind trapped in a body and only half of the body moved. I thought of those who looked at me with knowing eyes but became so frustrated when they could not speak any words clearly. I remembered some of my women patients and the anguish they experienced when they realized they had the "big C: in their breast and that surgery to cut out the cancer was what they faced. Not exactly like having your tonsils removed, since this was removing all of part of an external body part that society uses to denote you as a desirable female. Everyone wants to be desired.

A hole in my head and a lump in my breast. The phrase skittered across my brain again, and I conjured up a pretty funny-looking me. At first, I started chuckling under my breath. The chuckle progressed to chuckling out loud, which progressed to a full-blown belly laugh. The uncontrollable tears rolling down my face were from the laughter, and it felt good.

I realized once again that I had been taught another lesson in the presence of a miracle. Way back on Christmas Day, I could have been yanked out of this world with no other breath to draw, no other tear to cry, and no other laughter. I did not know what the outcome of my repeat mammogram would show, but no matter…I would live today. I would live it as if it were my last day, last hour, or last minute on this earth. Never again would I take this mortal life so seriously, for this life is but a vapor. Oh, how true that is. I knew and believed that the Creator who had breathed the breath of life into me could stop me from drawing the next one in the blink of an eye, if that was the plan. I also knew that each moment, hour, and day lived with our family and friends on this earth were truly gifts. I have never been one to turn down a gift, so I decided to live, laugh, and wait for the results.

Not many days and lots of laughter following my revelation, the phone rang. I grabbed it and heard my doctor's voice. The news was great! Whatever had been seen in the first mammography was not seen in the second one. I can honestly say that I know firsthand that, "Yea, though I walk through the valley of the shadow of death, I will fear no evil, for thou art with me."

Conclusion

If you have made your way to this point, you may think that the rational, responsible adult I referred to in the beginning has taken some circumstances in life and called them miracles. Stay with me just a little longer.

While riding in my car one evening, I heard a story on some Christian radio station that touched me. I do not know the author or the man who relayed the story, but it went something like this.

There was a man who had always tried to live a good life and do what was right. All of a sudden, he noticed that he was having trouble with his head. He was having thoughts he shouldn't have. Before long he noticed that his hands were doing things he knew they shouldn't do. Soon his feet were taking him places where he knew he shouldn't go. Finally, he gave up and went to see his physician, Dr. Law. He told his doctor that he was having this trouble with his head his hands and his feet. He wasn't thinking, doing, or going where he knew he should. Dr. Law checked him over and said, "You have a problem with your heart."

The man responded, "My heart! No! It's a problem with my head, my hands and my feet."

Dr. Law assured him, "No, you have a problem with your heart."

"Can you fix it?"

"No, but you should go see Dr. Grace. He can take care of your problem."

"How do I get an appointment?"

"You don't need one. Just go down the hall and knock on the door marked Dr. Grace."

The man did as he was told and heard a voice call, "Come in."

Dr. Grace asked about the problem. The man proceeded to tell him that he had a problem with his head, hands, and feet, but that Dr. Law had sent him because he thought he had a heart condition that only he, Dr. Grace, could fix. The man then asked how much the procedure would cost. Dr. Grace assured the gentleman that he could not pay the price because it had already been paid in full

Dr. Grace then examined the man and said, "Yes, you have a heart problem, and if we don't fix it, you will die. Do you want me to fix your heart problem?"

Understanding that the full price had been paid and if he didn't get his heart fixed he would surely die, the man asked Dr. Grace to go ahead and fix his heart. With that simple invitation, Dr. Grace reached inside the man's chest and removed a hard, blackened, and sinful heart. Dr. Grace replaced the old heart with a soft, warm one, overflowing with the love of God and the promise of life.

If you've not seen any miracles, perhaps you haven't met the Miracle Maker. Please take a short journey with me. First, find a New Testament; then turn to the book of Romans and read:

>Romans 3:23
>Romans 5:8, 12
>Romans 6:23
>Romans 10:9—10, 13

If you understand these verses and ask Dr. Grace (Jesus) to fix your heart, you have become a child of God. You now have the faith of a child. You have met the Miracle Maker; and I assure you, if you listen, look and believe, he will also let you have a peek through the pearlies and see the promise of the life to come.

www.ingramcontent.com/pod-product-compliance
Lightning Source LLC
LaVergne TN
LVHW020439080526
838202LV00055B/5264